THAT GAY CHRISTIAN GIRL

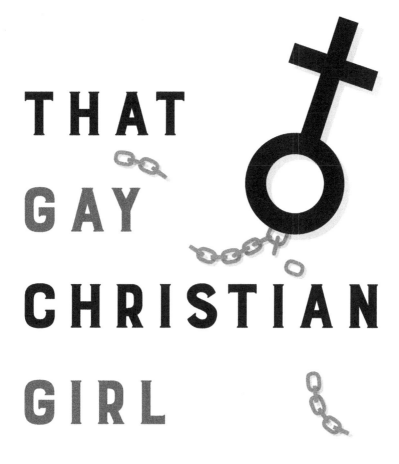

Everyone deserves love

Poems by

CERENA ORTIZ

Designed by Clare Baggaley at www.clarebaggaley.graphics
Edited by Lisa Edwards

This book is dedicated to:

Those who feel alone in their walk of life.
Those who seek God and feel conflicted.
Those who struggle with loving themselves.

EVERYONE.

DESERVES.

LOVE.

CONTENTS

TO MY FELLOW CHRISTIANS...13

DEAR GAY PEOPLE...14

WELCOME TO MY CHILDHOOD...19

NAVY DAYS PART 1...33

VIRGINIA BEGINNINGS
NAVY DAYS PART2...41

LOVING LYLA
NAVY DAYS PART3...61

TRUTH SET FREE...131

TO CONCLUDE...162

ACKNOWLEDGEMENTS...168

LOVE

I was young when I began writing. My second-grade teacher assigned poems for us students to memorize and perform in front of the class. I always enjoyed these poems and found comfort in the stories they told. I began trying to do it myself. It wasn't until the seventh grade that I realized that I had been given a means to express myself. I wrote so much that I felt that I was unlocking different worlds that existed inside of me.

I wrote about all the feelings and thoughts that I didn't feel safe to share with anyone else. My journals became my best friends. I could tell them anything without judgment. Each page, a blank canvas for me to create on. I could express how sad and confused I was. I could write about my anger towards God and my fear of hell. And I did. The more I wrote, the more I grew to understand myself because I was never afraid to see myself. However, accepting myself was a completely different story.

This book consists of a series of narratives, in consecutive order. Brief, important moments of my life. Following these narratives are poems and thoughts from my journals. They share my emotions and the different states of mind that I was in during each of these times.

Oh,

    To that little girl that I used to be.

If only I could have eased your worries.
If only I could have told you
  that Mom and Dad
    will always love you.
If only I could have damned your fears
  and told you that you have never been,
and never will be,
an abomination
or disgusting
before the eyes of God!

But you'll see...
  You'll see...
how I've grown to be here for you,
and how much I've grown to truly love you.
I'm sorry,
  so, so sorry,
That it took me so long...

TO MY FELLOW CHRISTIANS,

First and foremost, I would like to thank those of you that have, unconditionally, loved me. I am thankful to God for putting you in my life. You've comforted me, prayed endlessly with and over me, lifted me up when I was low, and gave me hope in the days that I prayed for death. Even though most of you didn't understand my struggle, you were listening and gave me non-judgmental ears to vent to. I don't think I could ever express my gratitude, but thank you once again.

As for the others, I ask you to read these words and try to see my story as the story of someone you are well-acquainted with; as someone you love, sharing this with you for the first time. I know that many of you don't understand, and that may not be your fault. You were raised by parents and a culture that did not bring you up to understand people from a different circle. However, some of you choose to remain ignorant with no attempt to understand and love someone who differs from you. But here, I offer my story to you. If I were to say that I am not anticipating judgment from you, I would be lying.

I am not here to make any truth claims other than the fact that I am Loved by God. And, I deserve to celebrate that without feeling shame, just as you do. I am not here to have or start any theological debates. I am simply writing about the experience of being myself.

DEAR GAY PEOPLE,

Many of you have suffered through similar journeys, if not worse ones than my own. Some of you have been shamed by Christians and people of other religions as well. I do not blame those of you who have walked away from faith; in fact, I attempted to do the same. There is so much pain when we are made to concentrate on just how short we fall instead of focusing on the Love of the Father. But it's not God that we tend to focus on when we come the conclusion to leave our faith, it's the people who drive us away. I completely understand that.

Some of you never did believe and don't have any desire to, and I get that as well. Why would you be drawn to people that condemn you and tell you that you're going to hell anyway? It's kind of a big turn off. It is very hard to focus on the possibility of there being a God that Loves you when the people who represent Him, here on Earth, won't give you the light of day or treat you like you're inferior.

With that said, I've failed to convince myself that He isn't real. I feel Him when I pray and when my favorite number, 44, comes up. When I worship him, I feel like there is nothing that can give me greater satisfaction. He overwhelms me with Love and beauty. I wish I could give you more to go off, but that's a walk only you can experience for yourself. No one can give you faith or make you believe.

I'm not here to convince you that God is real. I'm just wanting to say that coming out as a Christian to some of you, was equally as hard as coming out as gay to Christians. I am judged on both sides.

If we want Christianity to be more open to accepting and understanding us, we too have to acknowledge that they haven't experienced or been exposed to a different culture other than the ones they were raised in. Don't be one-sided or hypocritical with the standards that you set for people who don't understand us.

For some people, its a series of events that occur before they stop and try to remember where it began... when it was, exactly, that their life was completely thrown off-track. For others, it is an exact moment, a specific event that took place, where they knew how different their lives would be.

For me, it was the latter.

She was seven

and I was six.

It must had been around eleven

that morning

when she came walking in.

I remember the way she walked

... as if she were a ballerina,

on the tips of her toes.

I remember the way her curls bounced

as she pranced out the door and

forever engraved,

stained,

in my mind.

It was the beginning of a new chapter

disguised

as a beautiful,

cheerful

little girl.

~~~~~~~

I never wanted them to know it,

but I grew up a little more that day.

It was the end of simple decisions.

It was the end of my life that I had known

... just the moment prior.

I was now a little girl,

broken into a sequence of questions.

~~~~~~~~~~~~~~~~~~~~~~~~~

WELCOME TO MY CHILDHOOD.

My walk with God has been anything but easy.

Elementary, middle, and high school me was so scared that she was going to hell simply because she was attracted to women. I never shared my feelings with anyone during those times.

Just God.

I used to pray all of the time to make up for the "evil" that was inside me. Could you imagine? A little girl begging God not to send her to hell for something she had no control over, something she couldn't even understand yet. Please, imagine that being your child…

Often, I would think back to the time, in my first-grade classroom, when I saw my first crush for the first time. It would give me great anxiety. I started suffering frequent panic and anxiety attacks. My mom would take me to our family doctor to address the pains in my chest. I didn't know what anxiety or panic was at the time. I told my mom that it must have been my heart. You see, I had Kawasaki's disease when I was much younger and insisted that my heart was still hurting. And it was, in so many ways.

I believed that I had no choice as to what direction my life would take. Relationships were always out of the question for me, no matter how I truly felt. That mentality and outlook about my sexuality trickled into so many different aspects of my self-perception. I was never good enough in my own eyes, so I became relatively good at self-discipline, to the point that I loved when I wanted something really bad just so that I could tell myself "no" … whether it be a cookie or love. I believed that over time God would see how badly I wanted to go to heaven and He would change me. But, He never did.

All those years I was trying to win God over by taking up my cross and denying myself the way that I thought I was supposed to, all I was doing was training myself to let people walk all over me and never trust any judgment that came from myself. I truly believed that my heart was broken: if it was broken, how could I possibly trust it to lead me? Although it did lead me to a very prayerful life, the intentions behind it were fueled by fear instead of being led by love. And let me tell you, nothing good was produced from my fear. It blinded me from seeing and accepting the fact that God already Loved me.

As I grew up, I heard the other kids start to gossip about who was gay and what their parents said about people like that. I still remember when I heard the term "gay" for the first time, in fourth grade. I couldn't believe there was something to describe what I was, but it made me feel like an alien, like I was less human. High school proved to be the worst experience. I did have the typical high-school fan club; by fan club, I mean people who liked to make it clear just how insignificant I truly was. Me trying to figure out my salvation just added a cherry on top of all of that, as I'm sure you can imagine.

My prayers grew to be more along the lines of accepting that God wasn't going to change me and that if He wanted me to carry on with my life the way I was, I would do it. But in my early twenties I followed that up with begging Him to take me out of my misery. I even grew confident that he would. I was so sure that I told my mom that I was probably going to die of cancer, or something. But as you're reading this, you can see that I am still very much alive. I eased my worries by clinging to the fact that I could trust God to not let me suffer for too long.

I used to hear so many people say that the good die young, and I was convinced that I knew why: it was because they gave themselves completely up and God saw their endurance and tolerance for their own sufferings. So, He took them to heaven because they had won the race, fought an amazing fight or something along those lines.

How innocent and naive, I was. I had crushes here and there during high school, but I learned to ignore them and tell myself that it was the devil that was trying to tempt me. I was on a mission to be seen by God for my willingness to fight; I was on a mission to die young. Little did I know, I was just a regular teen. Go figure! Yet there I was, readying myself to die. People used to ask me if I was afraid of death, and I always said no. They would look at me but could never possibly see the pain that had made a home for itself inside the depths of my blood and mind. They couldn't have known that I was looking forward to the day that I didn't have to put up a front and that I craved to feel the relief of not being on this planet anymore. No one would have ever known: I was always smiling, laughing, super-active, and I loved my family.

However, I had no confidence in myself and I could not stress to you how badly I wished God would remove me from the rest of history.

I don't understand,

Father.

If it's true

that you hate me,

why would you create me?

And if you don't hate me,

   why would you create me

      like this?

Only to condemn me.

~~~~~~~~~~~~~~~~~~

I hurt,

  I hurt deep.

I can't reach ... the pain in the pit of me.

Maybe if I cry enough

  it will surface like a diamond in the rough...

or maybe I can make something of myself

and maybe the pain will subside.

I wonder what David felt

when he cried, "Hallelujah!"

I didn't know my demons could draw those words from me,

just as easily as my lungs release...

"Hallelujah..."

Can you hear the beauty in this ache?

What do I know about a true "Hallelujah"?

I'm drowning beneath the illusion.

~~~~~~~~~~~~~~~~~~~~~

Chase my dreams
  and follow my heart?
But how could I?

If they only knew the truth,
  they would know that I'm broken,
and my dreams must be wicked.
They would know
  that my compass
  ... points me to hell
and I'm incapable
 of Love.

If I can't trust my own heart to lead me,
then whom can I trust?
Where then,
  am I safe?

~~~~~~~~~

Since I am attracted to girls, I find myself wondering if the only difference is the way girls look, and of course the body parts. How the eyes of the flesh betray us.

I began to think about people as if I were blind. What would I focus on about a person to determine what they meant to me? I found that "she" was the one to show understanding and patience. "She" was more emotionally awakened and wild beneath the calm that society had clothed her with. "She" knew what it meant to be a woman and to love. "He" always had to be right and in charge. "He" didn't know what it was to have to try to belong in our cultural mandates, so he couldn't understand me. I felt alone with men, and I felt more seen and awakened with women. It had little to do with how a soul looked, rather, it was about how a soul felt. The beauty and appeal of women was just the cherry on top.

Like a prison

my mind governs me.

All of my dreams and fantasies,

   visions,

glimpses of wishes, chained,

blamed by my conscience

   like a bitch,

      or a spineless Mrs.

But how long can I ignore an itch?

A question only patience can answer,

   but even the flesh wears thin.

Or ... is strength all that matters?

~~~~~~~~~~~~~~~~~~~~~~~~~~~~~~~~~~

From the ends of my fingers
    to the tips of my toes,
from the so-called "counted" hairs on my head
    to the "never-to-be-stricken" flesh of my feet,
somewhere in between
    exists ... me.
I find myself examining my reflection,
    searching my eyes,
        trying
to find the life ... in me.

~~~~~~~~~~~~~~~~

Can we go on an adventure that transcends our thoughts?

Our minds aren't free here.

~~~~~~~~~~~~~~~~

If I'm an abomination,

    then what of me is worth a sense of purpose?

~~~~~~~~~~~~~~~~~~~~~~~~~~~~~~~~~~~

I'm hiding,

    but am I denying myself well enough?

What purpose is there in running?

Where is the balance?

Would they reject me if I didn't reject myself?

I hid behind a facade,

    a mask ...

        all of my life.

Am I going to make it out of all of this?

~~~~~~~~~~~~~~~~~~~~~~~~~~~~~~~~~~~

I have yet to cave into society.

    I've been left scared shitless

        to live life to the fullest.

I've been running from myself,

    living life to the upmost propriety.

Now it feels like everything is building up,

piles upon piles of anxiety.

Is it Christian life

    or is it stupidity?

Here I am left to question.

~~~~~~~~~~~~~~~~

Am I allowed to question?

Is it ok to disagree,

    but to still obey?

Am I allowed,

    am I allowed to doubt

        all of reason?

Why was I given a life if

    I was not meant to govern it?

How can I speak of anything in first person,

    if I would be speaking in a lie?

As I obey,

    and even against myself,

why am I the one to deal with guilt and frustration?

And the ones who mock You,

    content and free of all,

        as they cave into temptation?

Father,

We both know that I can't do this.
We both know that I lack the discipline
     to follow Your commandments.
I obey the pain I feel from You.
It tells me to refrain
     and what tempts me,
          will flee.
But,
     it never leaves.

~~~~~~~~~~

God,

Take me in my youth,
     before I have the chance to stray from you.

~~~~~~~~~~

NAVY
DAYS

PART 1

At the age of sixteen, I decided I would join the Navy. At the age of seventeen, I convinced my parents to sign for me to leave for bootcamp just two weeks after high-school graduation. I was in desperate need to feel proud of something I'd done. I didn't have the issue of too much pride in my youth, although many people did think that I was boastful: it was just a front that I used as a mask. I thought that joining the service might help me; it would help me by giving me a way out. Maybe I would die. Maybe I would be taken somewhere far away without the means of returning. Or maybe I could find a way to find myself. The only thing that was certain to me, was that I just needed to leave. Every day I looked forward to when I would ship off to bootcamp and be given the opportunity to recreate myself in another life.

I remember that moment that everyone came to see me before my recruiter drove me to MEPS (Military Entrance Processing Station) to start my career. My whole family came, with the exception of my grandpa. He didn't believe that I was doing what was best for me, for more than one reason. But I knew that he had no idea what I was facing internally. He left his home at the age of twenty, in the early 1940s, and never turned back. All he saw in store for me was a great deal of loneliness and regret. I understood, and I believe he grew to understand, that times are different now.

My best friend of seven years at the time did attend my send-off. I had only seen her cry once before, and the day I left was the second. My father telling me that he loved me didn't help me with trying not to cry. You see, my dad isn't a very affectionate person: he shows his love through actions and making you laugh. He wasn't one for hugging or expressing himself through words, but that day, he pulled me in close and told me that he loved me. To this day, it is the first time that I can recall him saying those words to me.

I always knew my mom would cry once I left. She was always

the one that I related to best. She understood my depth and reciprocated her own with what I did share with her throughout my childhood. There was so much love in the air that morning.

As I got in the car, I looked at everyone standing outside. Slow motion, everything moving so slowly ... as if time were giving me one last chance to change my mind. I felt a huge sense of loss, as well as so much relief. I felt conflicted but knew what I had to do. I turned to face forward and I didn't look back once I'd locked my eyes on the scene through the windshield. I couldn't help but think of the new journey that I was now on. I prayed to God continuously, to never remove His hand from what was to come.

Once in bootcamp, I met so many people from different backgrounds and different places that I was in culture shock. We were different ages and different races; we had different talents and different beliefs – some of which I'd never even thought about.

And, there were many other gay people. I found myself so intrigued by them and their confidence; they owned themselves without a second thought. I wasn't attracted to them, I just wanted to know how they were able to get through life. I needed to know. It would be many years later before I discovered how...

I went to school in Florida and then got stationed on an aircraft carrier in Virginia. Virginia – this was the place where I grew the most, spiritually and mentally. I was on a journey to self-discovery. My faith and my relationship with God skyrocketed. I was so filled with His Love and craved to know Him more. I thought that I had discovered what my purpose was; all I needed was God.

I didn't want a relationship with anyone, I wanted life to just consist of me and Him. At the time, I couldn't imagine wanting it any other way, but, I still needed to confront myself. When I did decide to try and get a better understanding of the secret parts of myself, I fell into it so hard. There was one girl that I became unhealthily stuck on. She was, and remains, the star of one of the biggest lessons of my life. But we'll get to that later.

These next seven years consisted of so many different highs and lows; days of deep friendships and periods of great loneliness. God became my first love, and my first heartbreak.

All of the years that compiled the first quarter of my life were painted with so much fear that it caused me to hallucinate, wet my bed, and have a sea full of doubt to drown myself in.

I can't help to think about what my life might bring,
  if I were to spill...
What would I unleash?
What space would I fill?
Beneath...

I am a different world,
  a saturated frenzy;
a vast, deep
foreign sea.

If I were to be inside out
  my skin would be lost within the
... endless abyss
of the reality that I've created.

~~~~~~~~~~~~~~~~~~~~~

Abuelito,

And I wasn't there.

  You told me that I wouldn't be,
but I hoped for the better.
Now,

  I'm racing through "what ifs"
and memories of you telling me this:
"Family is the most important thing."
You told me that's all I'd be learning.
You're gone now...

  and I'm wishing I had the chance

    to tell you that there is more to the story.
Only if you could see me growing.
I feel I understand the ways in which you were brought up,
and I respect them.
From that time,

  I see the world changing;
it's ageing,
rearranging for the better

  and worse.

But I choose to add to the good.

I wish you could see the role I play...

    It's like I'm an instrument of the choirs of heaven

contributing to a good song.

And although I may hiccup,

    and I may play a note wrong,

He still chooses to use me.

You see,

    there is no motive,

        no reason for me ... to hide.

~~~~~~~~~~~~~~~~~~~~~~~~~~~~~

I don't like to walk on pavements.

They give me no sense of adventure.

~~~~~~~~~~~~~~~~~~~~~~~~~~~~~

At times,

I wonder what it is

that opens up inside of me.

Within,

   there is knowledge

     and a truth.

It lies deep

   and it lies in a whisper.

I don't know where inside of me

   that this logic resides.

If not my heart nor mind,

   what else inside can be so vast?

~~~~~~~~~~~~~~~~~~~~~~~~

VIRGINIA BEGINNINGS

NAVY DAYS

PART 2

My first year living in Virginia was filled with so much love.

I tried to make friends with the fellow sailors, but I found myself to have very little in common with the majority of them. When we did hang out, our time together consisted of them drinking and talking about their crushes and who they'd slept with. The conversations and the alcohol always seemed to make me quite uncomfortable back then. I felt completely out of place and more alone than I already did. So I dedicated myself to finding another way to occupy my time.

I started coaching an under-14 travel softball team. Although I was just the assistant, it took up so much of my time. I enjoyed mentoring and coaching these younger ladies. They were spunky, energetic, and always kept me amazed by how weird they were (in a good way). I guess I was more comforted being around a more innocent crowd.

During my time coaching, we worked a bingo hall on Saturdays to raise money for tournaments and uniforms. I didn't mind spending all of my day there. I felt that I had a purpose, and that's all I really need for me to truly enjoy something. One Saturday, a basketball team joined us and we were now teaching them how to work the bingo hall. The senior citizens could be a little feisty at times, from what I remember. Anyway, there was this fifteen-year-old girl there that was really quiet: her name was Molly. She seemed cool and collected, and was so young. I kept thinking, how can a fifteen-year-old walk around with that much confidence? She drew me in with her calm assurance. Or, maybe it was envy. I can't remember how we got talking, but we did. I was telling her that I was relatively new to Virginia. She asked me if I found a church that I liked yet. She went on to talk about her church and how amazing it was. To my luck, the church wasn't far from where I was living in town at the time, so she invited me and I accepted. I continued to go to that church for all of my remaining years in Virginia. Molly's family took me in and treated me kindly. Being there gave me a great sense of family and deeper connection. I loved it! And soon enough, I didn't feel so lonely anymore.

I cannot begin to tell you how much more profound and real my relationship with God grew to be. I fell in love in a way that I never knew possible. Worship became like air to me; reading my Bible became like my new chocolate addiction; praying became as natural as breathing. I felt like I never wanted to stop praying! From the second I said "God" in my head, I could feel a current, like a literal current around me. He was so evident in my life, there was nothing that I wanted, only Him. My friends showed me so much beauty, so much music and time dedicated to be together in His presence. Like, worship was what we did for fun! I still miss those days, to be honest.

The Bible studies and Sunday sermons kept me fed spiritually but also kept me hungry for more. I grew to believe that the only thing worth paying attention to was God; questions pertaining to Him were simply the only things worth pondering and talking about. I didn't see how my peers around me could be so shallow and uncurious about the actions of God and eternal life. I needed answers on what was to come of me, and I felt like I was in the right spot to find them. But the more I focused on what I thought I needed to be, the less I paid attention to my friends outside of church. I surrounded myself with the people that I wanted, so badly, to be like. I never considered who I was supposed to be and I didn't like who I was becoming.

If a flame

    could feel,

it wouldn't need the wind.

    It would find a way to grow feet

and ...

it would chase what it craved,

    what it burned for.

If a flame had a name,

    or a place

        where it'd be forever safe,

it would be called Passion,

    and you would find it

somewhere inside this flesh of mine.

~~~~~~~~~~~~~~~~~~~~~~~~~~~~~~~~~~

Have you ever let yourself feel the wind,
    by breathing it in with all your being?
Have you ever cared to just let it caress you and push
    your tears behind you?
Are you afraid to let it sweep you off your feet?

~~~~~~~~~~~~~~~~~~~~~~~~~~~~~~~~

It goes deeper still,
    but what kind of power does this?
Lungs of bliss;
    a tongue's new language.
What kind of change renders limits
... boundless,
but, goes deeper still?
    How to explain
        what it is that I am feeling...

~~~~~~~~~~~~~~~~~~~~~~~~~~~~~~~~

How wild and free are thee

O' Lord?

I feel you in the wind...

I see you when I look into a friend's eyes...

I hear you when the ocean roars...

  God, my God,

    you have no limitations.

Where is it that you allow me to go within the

    depths of creation?

The place I drift to where my feet are useless...

~~~~~~

Many truths are birthed into this world
with pangs of pain.

    They are born as children of our life lessons
and we tend to nurture them

    and raise them up as forts to protect us from deceit.
There ... are many "truths".

But God,

    Yours is the only one that matters;
Yours is the only fort built with everlasting Truth;
Yours is the only one built on solid ground

    where I can rest and feast,
even in the midst of my enemies.

~~~~~~~~~~

I used to ask the wind if it lives.
I never heard the answer,
but it continued to move.
Gently, it would caress my curiosity;
with bliss,
it would embrace my flesh.
What more should I need?

~~~~~~~~~~

O' God of Jacob

God of me,

unblind my eyes;

    help me to see

        everything you need me to be in this world.

And I know the only way is to let myself go,

    so humble me,

        bring me to my knees,

Let my tears fall like heaven's rain

    only in the praise of Your sweet name,

so I can be free,

forever and inevitably,

    in the presence of Your Grace.

Help me to grow to be more like You,

and when temptation comes about my days,

    remind me of the innocence upon Your face.

I wish only to be in Love with You

    in the more permanent phase!

~~~~~~~~~~~~~~~~

Bare feet...
Gravity grounds you
    against and through
the moon's cold creek.

I beg of you...
Step-weary.
You
    hold my soul...
Beyond's antique.

So
as the night's song
strums through the atmosphere
upon the river's gentle current…
From the wolverine's howl
    owning the crisp air...
The very same,
I inhale,
keep to your step without a yield!

Walk my troubled flesh into
the valley's numbing water.

Take four steps,

then

one more,

and

on that fifth

aim my image

    downstream, in its spirit's core.

And this

... this moment, is where I bid you

stop!

and goodbye.

Oh,

but stay and watch.

Without you,

my calloused feet…

The river's current

    sweeps

    and pulls me under.

But my soul's faith

like an anchor,

and to the bottom

    I sink.

And run down rocks
   where I lay my head,
and for the night becomes my bed.

Without a second,
with no time to close my eyes,
blurred images
   through moving water
become my sight.

Hushed are my thoughts,
and in this
   new,
   profound silence,
filtered is my mind.

Washed
am I,
cleansed
am I,
And He is here now
   telling me,
"Rise!"

So

    I do not hesitate

to obey.

But this time

help is not necessary

from you, old feet.

You,

    who were once my roots.

He gave me wings!

I have never needed

    anything

    of this world,

but always

    desired it all.

Which is why

    I bid you

goodbye!

You,

my bare feet,

You!

    who left my trace

upon the Earth's ageing skin,

Only so that temptation

    could track me.

But with wings,

    only

God! can find me.

~~~~~~~~~~~~~~~~

The walls were rivers.

Forever, they seemed to persist,

   like space and sky.

Like God, with endless life they pursued to consist!

But what was my purpose in between vertical waters?

There was no beginning,

   there was no end.

There was ground and rivers up.

So I walked

   and as I did so,

the walls whispered through the hushes of roaring waters.

"Why move and not observe?"

Chilling echoes through soft choirs

   they sounded to me!

And so I stopped,

though the current continued to flow.

   Only the moment I was able to cease,

   and in that moment

I knew nothing was needed but serenity,

   so I let it give me peace!

And from there on,

   I refused to waste another breath until I was ready to observe,

ready to see all the wonder the voices were preparing me

   to perceive.

And as I chose to breathe,

to signify I was ready,

the spirit of the rivers hit me

like a gust of wind and ripped me open

only to hit me again,

to restore my sight with new eyes from its everlasting life.

And let me tell you,

then I could see!

With all I wish I could share

because with words alone,

I'd be known to be deranged,

crazy!

If only Immaculacy could be seen by all eyes.

Could you imagine the purity in a complexion...?

All differences would be allies.

If only you could be where I was in that moment.

If only the rivers would you consume your world

and bless you with these eyes.

The ability to separate all Truth and lies,

would be yours!

~~~~~~~

If His words were the sea

    you're resting on the surface,

        while the Truth lies in the deep.

So, why do you stay at the top,

    only so your flesh can breathe?

Let me ask you,

    how long can you hold your breath?

~~~~~~~~~~~~~~~~~~~~~~~~~~~~~~

When I pray

... I sit in light.
  At times, I stand,
  at times, I bow.
But in light,
  I remain,
For He is Light,
I AM is He!

It is endless...
  There is nothing it cannot hold.
  There is nothing to which it would fold.
It is my sanctuary,
  my tabernacle,
He is my haven!

~~~~~~~~~

What is my way?
What is my path if not Your voice?

~~~~~~~~~

I can love the world
    but I know I'm not living
    'til I'm loving You.
Oh ...
    loving You
is what I'm meant to do.

~~~~~~~~~~~~

I may be young,
I have not quite yet bloomed
    for my season has not yet come.
But still,
    some things I am able to perceive,
and other truths,
    I pursue and I'm learning.

But the reason for complacency in ignorance

... I cannot grasp

Life itself, love itself, reason itself

    is pushed aside.

And for what?

To temporarily satisfy your hunger for

    self-satisfaction?

We are so quick to confront the world

    and demand what we want before

        we ever confront ourselves.

I guess it is scary

    to admit to, and face the shame we carry.

But ignorance is not bliss,

    and selfish ambition

        does lead to a road of death.

... I'd rather seek than to never find.

~~~~~~~~~~~~~~~~~~~~~~~~

Is it that hard to control yourself,

to set aside your own needs or the temporary things you

want, for that matter?

because all of your regrets come from within,

and never from He who leads.

And as you ignore Him and do as you please,

temptation will grow like weeds.

And because we are weak

we cry and we water them

with tears of our own self-pity!

~~~~~~~~~~~~~~~~~~~~~~~~

LOVING
LYLA

NAVY DAYS

PART 3

Where did my inspiration go off to? I feel lost without the creativity. I feel lost without possibilities knocking on the door to my mind! What consumes my thoughts and energy, and refuses to free me from its captivity?

I'm ready to feel something again. I'm ready to live with peace, in my freedom. Why can't I just have that already?

All I want is love. I know I tell people otherwise, but I crave a love. I crave a kiss I will not grow tired of; eyes that couldn't possibly feel warmer on my flesh; a heart that yearns to truly see, as much as me.

So there I was, onboard the USS *Dwight D. Eisenhower* CVN69 (an aircraft carrier), placed in dry dock in Portsmouth, VA in 2015. We were in the shipyards at the time. I was assigned to verifying tag-outs throughout the ship; these were little ticket-shaped tags that came in different colors, used to mark the inoperability of a piece of equipment. At times, it truly felt like a hunt. It was quite the chore, mainly just tedious. But I hated sitting still so I always volunteered to get up and do it. I was able to spend hours out of my workspace to walk around and think about whatever I wanted. It was my favorite part of those months that we were under construction.

There was nothing out of the ordinary that Monday. I, once again, volunteered to verify the tag-outs and was beginning my journey throughout the ship. I was walking aft, towards the back of the ship, in the hangar bay when I saw her.

Lyla.

Have you ever seen a stranger that made you believe that you were meant to meet? Well, that was her. I don't know how to explain it, but I felt her somehow. I stopped in my tracks so I could get a longer look at her walking towards and past me. Lyla didn't see me, but I watched her the whole time (not to sound like a creep).

The way she walked was so confident, yet humble. There was a simplicity to her. She had perfect, olive skin. Her hair, just as dark as mine, was up in a perfect sock-bun. She had no parting in her hair, which kind of bothered me, but she was still so beautiful. The expression on her face was almost stoic: no smile or grin; no sense of anger, just strength. Maybe she was lost in thought. I thought about what she could be thinking about and where she was going. I looked forward to when it was that I would see her again.

It wasn't too long before I did.

I had a work acquaintance, Rachel, who asked if I wanted to work out with her a couple of days later that week. I was excited to spend time with her, but I did think it was a bit odd since she had never reached out before. Rachel insisted on driving out to the barracks that I was assigned to since we had a pretty decent gym there. I just thought she was trying to be nice at the time, but when I walked into the gym, she informed me that she'd invited someone else that lived in the same place as me. I told her that I didn't mind. She pointed over by the far, right, corner of the gym and there, there stood the beginning of a new chapter for me.

It was Lyla.

I know how odd it sounds, but for some reason I already felt like she was mine. It made no sense to me. At this point in my life, I was committed to a life of abstinence and without any romantic relationships. So, how on earth was it, that I could feel so confident in thinking that Lyla and I belonged to each other? I approached her as if I expected for her to feel the same. Stupid me! But she was nice enough. The three of us worked out together and had dinner – it was a great night for me. However, I was oblivious to the relationship between the two of them.

I didn't know anything until the next night.

Lyla had texted me after work the next day to ask if I wanted to work out again; Rachel was to be on duty. Duty days consist of at least twenty-four hours onboard the ship, so there was no way for her to join us. Of course, I agreed to the two of us spending time together without Rachel. Instead of working out, we decided to go rollerblading around the barracks for a while. I was clearly the one who was better at rollerblading, but Lyla was so intriguing to be around.

There was a parking garage in the barracks complex where we lived. We went up to the fifth floor to enjoy the view of the lights from the military airfield. We talked for a while. I immediately opened up to her about being into girls and about how I felt so conflicted about it because of my faith. She wasn't much of a talker, but I felt like she was genuinely interested in what I believed and my story. She sat there, on top of the edge of the parking garage, nothing but moonlight above her head, her feet dangling above the ground in those black and red roller blades, her hair still in the military-styled bun from work, and her eyes just looking at me while I rolled around on the cement in front of her. I couldn't tell what she was thinking, but I felt something I had never felt before that moment.

I wanted to kiss her.

We chose to head back to her room to make dinner. Rolling down the ramps of the parking garage took an unexpected turn for me. I wasn't ready to be tempted any further. But going down one of the ramps, Lyla took a pretty good fall and scraped her shin. She was bleeding but made it seem like it was something to laugh at, so I didn't make a big deal out of it. I rolled over to her and extended my hand down to help her up. She grabbed it and pulled herself up into me, with her other hand going around my waist. Her face was so close to mine, I could almost breathe her in. I don't know if she just needed some extra balance, but feeling her so close to me, even if it was for just a split second, sent fireworks throughout my body and mind. I grew scared of where the night would go.

Lyla cooked that night: chicken, rice and broccoli. It was a typical meal we had after a workout. She brought out some wine and we drank a little bit. In the meantime, she talked briefly about Rachel and their friendship. She admitted to them being a little more than friends, but assured me that there was no title for what they were. It saddened me to hear because I didn't want to hurt Rachel, but I felt that Lyla was mine.

After talking for a while, I thought it would be more comfortable to lay down on the carpet of the living room. Call me weird, but I still do that to this day – I find it comfy. Anyway, I had begun to doze off when Lyla woke me up and told me that I could just stay there for the night if I wanted. I thanked her and accepted the offer, fully intending to sleep in the living room. She turned off the lights and I sprung up: I was terribly afraid of the dark!

"Why don't you just sleep on the bed, dude?" Lyla asked me.

"I'm good in here, it's no big deal. Can't you just leave the lights on?"

Lyla laughed and turned the lights off. I jumped off the floor and went into her room. I was so silly, even just those few years ago: scared of the dark, scared of the physical, sensual touch of another; scared of her. At first I attempted to just lie down on the floor of her room, but she breathed out a sigh of annoyance and insisted on me just getting in her bed. I told myself I was probably just overthinking it, as I usually do.

I got in the far side of the bed, closest to the wall, trying to comfort myself with the thought of her just being any other friend. It didn't help – I felt so much tension between us. I was lying on my back, as was she. I closed my eyes and after a few minutes, I started to relax. And then a moment that was dripping with the beginning of so much promise for heartache began.

She kissed my shoulder.

"What are you doing?" I asked.

"Relax, I was just saying goodnight."

I took it for what she said. A few moments later, she kissed my cheek.

"What are you doing?" I asked again.

"It's just a kiss, it's no big deal."

My heart was racing uncontrollably, my head spinning, and every part of my body felt like I was melting. She was petrifying me – I couldn't move. Even though I was scared, I was also curious. I wanted her to do whatever it was that was supposed to happen next.

"What are you thinking about?" Lyla asked, as if she didn't know already. I wanted so badly not to want her...

"I'm thinking about how I don't want to kiss you," I replied, reluctantly, honestly.

She reached across my body and grabbed my shoulder to pull herself on top of me. She kissed me.

We made out that night, but nothing more. It was slow. Her lips, naturally the color and feel of soft rose petals, were so gentle yet strong against mine. So much thought and emotion went into every kiss. The way I fell asleep in her arms that night felt like I fit so perfectly against her. As I grew sleepy, I remember trying to stay awake just so I could be conscious of the fact that she was holding me.

But the next day, I cried. I cried so much. After working on the ship and feeling all the shame and confliction from the forbidden feelings that I had suppressed for so long, I became too tired.

When I got back to the barracks from work, I sat in my car for four hours. It felt like a matter of minutes. I started to pray, but even praying didn't seem to console me. I felt like I'd failed a huge test: God's test. I had always prided myself on the fact that I was able to deny myself this. I had the discipline to refrain, even though it was hard. I thought I was so strong. How could this girl that I just met, make me fail? My whole relationship with God became questionable. I was immediately filled with more fear than I had ever experienced. And worst of all, I let that fear take the wheel of my relationship with my Heavenly Father.

All the time I was chasing Lyla, throwing myself at her even, she remained in a "non-relationship" with Rachel. Yes, it was weird. And no, I wouldn't count it as my proudest moment. We didn't tell Rachel anything about it for about two years.

I grew to know Lyla very well – her interests complimented mine; our thoughts seemed to bounce off each other's. I loved how she dedicated herself to self-growth and deep thinking. She made me feel alive through conversation alone and inspired me to seek out more for my life. Although our relationship was mainly a one-sided friendship that I was too blind to see, I am certain that I would be a completely different person today without my time with her.

Rachel was always in the picture. She was so kind and loyal to Lyla and more than tolerant of me, but still I continued to mislead her. I can tell she didn't want me around as often as I was, but I was so fixated on being around Lyla that I didn't care. In my eyes, Lyla and Rachel were never going to make it because Lyla belonged with me. I wasn't even nervous about that aspect – it was all just a matter of time in my head.

I was definitely in a very different, unhealthy state of mind, but all I focused on was Lyla. My whole life became about Lyla. I still prayed and went to church. I still worshipped and asked God for guidance. But in retrospect, it was almost all in vain. I had no clue as to just how mentally unhealthy I was.

You see, Lyla was probably the only person who knew me. I didn't ever have any secrets from her. She *was* my secret, and I clung so hard to her. I believe that's why I wanted her so badly. She knew me and didn't see an issue: well, other than the fact that I can be a little bit overbearing. But I had no guard up when I was around her. I was able to just be me and not have to wonder how to hide. I gave her too much power – power over me that she never even wanted.

Because she never wanted me.

But I did love her.

Even though I still have love for her and feel that I always will, I know that we were toxic in each other's lives. I am completely at peace with wishing her well from a distance; she was never good for me and I believe it's safe to say that I was never good for her. I've grown to love and respect myself. Back then, I thought I had everything together, but I felt like between her and my relationship with God, I was shattered into a billion pieces that I had no clue how to put back together.

To make matters worse, as I opened up to the people at church, I felt them break away from me. Maybe it was a matter of coincidence – they remained cordial at Sunday service – but nothing was ever the same between us all. Looking back, I know that they must have thought it was just better to distance themselves because they had no idea how to interact with me. I just wish they had talked to me instead of making me feel like I had demons surrounding me. I tried and tried to spend time with them, but they moved further and further away from me. I even felt like God was neglecting me! The church not accepting me felt like God was saying that He didn't either. I blamed my first heartbreak on Him.

I was shattered

    from the second I saw you.

I watched you walking towards me

    and it feels like I've been trying

        to hold onto that moment.

But in reality,

    you walked past me.

I've been watching you walk away ever since.

You never noticed me;

    you walked straight past the pieces you shattered.

I've never moved,

    I remained ...

        hopeful,

praying that you'd turn around

    and see me too.

But I never did have a chance.

    I was only blessed with a brief vision

        of you.

I guess it's my turn

     to turn around

    and walk away

... who knows what's walking ahead.

I'm flooded with guilt right now! There is no desire to move from my car at the moment. I've been sitting here for four hours. All I can seem to do is write this and listen to Christian music. I feel so guilty that even the music adds to my guilt. I'm trying to think of why I feel guilty if I wanted to do what I did. I believe it's because I knew and told myself that it was wrong in more than two ways, yet I acted. The law's existence convicts me now. My own desires defile me, and therefore even myself I cannot trust. God! If You are here, then hear me Father. I need You...

Written after the first time I kissed Lyla.

Do you know that moment,
  that feeling when your flesh sings
as you satisfy it?
How good it feels,
   and you actually convince yourself to believe that
      that's what living is?
I lust for the freedom I feel in that moment.
Can you relate, are you familiar?
When your flesh sings and your soul cries, all at once.

Will this kill me?

Oh, Father,

   please have mercy,

'cause I'm finding myself dancing with the demons,

dancing away to the song of my inner passions.

Ahh, I know it's wicked,

   so why do I find such beauty in this pleasure?

Did I ever love you?

   I wanted so badly to love you!

Is my life nothing more than a kiss from Judas?

~~~~~~~~~~~~~~~~~~~~~~~~~~~~~~~~~~~

You're the forbidden fruit in my life
    the part that I'm supposed to deny,
the one thing I want
    that I shouldn't bite.
Must be why
    I'm terrified
... scared of always wanting you,
and scared of letting you go.
It's a high,
    knowing that fear is inevitable.
Which way will we roll the dice?
I think I like it ...
    this rollercoaster ride.

～～～～～～～

You're everything I never wanted.
    Yet,
        You're all I want.

～～～～～～～

Feelings that contradict
   the way I try to live
   pour straight down over me.
The world has finally
   discovered my weakness.
I try to hide
   but it turns out to be
   that I am already exposed.

~~~~~~~~~~~~~~~~~~~~~~~~

The greatest mysteries are
   beneath and beyond
   the surface of the sea.
So I'm told...
And yet,
   your eyes, deep,
   I find myself clueless in.

~~~~~~~~~~~~~~~~~~~~~~~~

What if I said
   I haven't seen the sky blue
   since you cut me off?

I think the blue fell from above
   and dressed me, sad.

～～～～～～～

No one knows,
   nobody really knows me.
A wasted passion
   burns inside of me.
Rivers of love
   flow through my veins.

Maybe my love is too heavy
   a burden to carry.
Maybe my touch
   is too much.

～～～～～～～

She watches me sleep, so simply.

Peacefully, I seem to sleep.

But she doesn't know what I see

in between my dreams

and her reality.

She doesn't know

and she'll never know ...

she'll never know.

~~~~~~~~~~~~~~~~~~~~

are always lost within the moments when my

alks along the outline of your brows,

too soon...

My fingertips grow jealous

of my eyes,

and I'm left with no choice but to trace your face with my

curious hands.

It's like ... they were shaped by winter itself.

There's a coolness to them

... an innocent frame

to encase the heat of your chaos,

'cause...

there's a mahogany flame that forts along the

circumference of your eyes...

It burns with intensity.

It burns beautifully.

You remind me of rain when the sun is still shining,

or snow days in my favorite coat ...

watching the fall of a frozen sky while I sip on hot chocolate.

Your eyes and brows,

they're like fire and ice.

~~~~~~~~~~~~~~~

Memories keep me guilty.

The night robs the light from my eyes
    and inhales my breath.
The wind steals my howl,
    steals my scream.
I'm numb in the night.
    I succumb.
I'm locked out from what's inside.

~~~~~~~~~~~~~~~~~~~~~~~~~

me to believe that it is all just a story?

me what is real?
Tell me what you see that is true?
Because it's clear to me that your green is my red,
your happiness is my death.
I know you think you're Switzerland,
    but I don't think those grounds exist in this war.
I see you willing to face persecution for the sake of who
    you are.
Can you teach me?
I don't believe I can make it very far.

~~~~~~~~~~~~~~~~~~~~~~~~~~~~

You'll never understand how much you made me love you.
And I'll never understand why you pushed me away.
I can't stay.

~~~~~~~~

Is it so wrong to believe

that you and me

could find ourselves in each other's arms?

'Cause I've seen diamonds

   surface from the deep,

secrets for us to keep.

And I know the love I'm looking for

   is only found where you are.

So tell me what your chains are?

What's holding you back

   from letting me see your heart?

~~~~~~~~~~~~~~~~~~~~~~~~~~~~~~~~

Who knew amethyst
   could be a liquid?
Like waves,
   your eyes invite me
   to explore the depths of you.
But truly,
   in the moonlight,
   the elements in your eyes gleam,
   like the howl of the wolverine.
How it captivates me in the night.

~~~~~~~~~~~~~~~~~~~~~~~~~~~~~~~~~~~~~~

This may escalate into
   something I'm afraid to do,
because the Truth offends
   and Love divides.
But I can see the light in the distance ...
   it's taking me away from you.

Cover the drains!

  Let's flood this place

  with all the Truth and Love in our blood.

Welcome the adrenaline building up in a rush.

Let's see who swims.

Truth offends the hearts that don't know Love,

  and Love divides the Truth from the lies.

So let's cover the drains

  and we'll see who will rise.

Don't let this offend you,

  don't let this divide us.

~~~~~~~~~~~~~~~~~~~~~~~

I was confused about my feelings towards Lyla. Some say that it was just lust that I was feeling. I mean, what was love if all that I was capable of was lust? I was always listening to everyone besides myself. I never acknowledged my feelings as something that was any good. I believed that the love that I felt was lust, because I thought that I was broken. But, I'm learning. My feelings were good. They were real. They were love, and still are. I never had anyone to help me to realize that, because I submerged myself in a culture that made me believe that the love I had was never love. But I loved Lyla, and still deeply care. It wasn't lust.

  I was attracted to her, yes, but out of the three and a half years of chasing her and another two of being on standby for her, we never slept together. I thought about the way that we would look at each other when we kissed. I yearned for and loved my place in her arms. I loved our silence in each other's company. I loved her disposition, her mentality, and how deeply she felt things, even if she never talked about them. Because when she did, those moments were priceless to me.

I know many Christian people believe that when you're attracted to someone of the same sex, that it is sinful and anything but love. But I know I love Lyla from the way that I wonder what she's doing: if she's ok; whether or not she's crying these days; if someone has hurt her. And when I think of her crying, my heart hurts and I wish I could just hold her. It breaks my heart at the thought of her feeling lonely. I know I love her from the way that I dream about her and from the way that I miss her. I know I love her from how much I pray for her. I've never prayed so much for a person.

She's beautiful, she's wild, she's driven and strong. She's judgmental but quiet; her skin is soft while her heart is calloused. It's never hard for her to find company, yet she's always lonely. It's her nature to be loved but to always push away.

You see, when I think of Lyla, I don't just think of her body. I think of her eyes and well-being. I just think of her, not sex. Just because I have feelings for her, does not make it lustful.

Should I be thankful for suffering?

Should I be thankful for the pain in my loneliness, for the fear of my fate?

When I was a little girl, I used to ask God to reveal the depths of me. I always felt so much more vast than my body could contain. I used to look and study my flesh and question how it was that everything that I felt within was able to dwell within my body. I always wondered about the capacity of my being.

Now, I see that I'm deeper than I was prepared for.

Deeper and darker.

Who am I to You, that You call?
What purpose am I to serve?
I feel myself growing distant, but it's like a line is attached to me and the other side, to You. That no matter how far I wander, we never lose each other. You above all, know that I am not a patient person, and still, there, You test me. I procrastinate, and still, You task me.

She lies through her eyes
    but her smile outshines.

Given the circumstances,
    is it ok to run?
Possibilities rest in peace behind me.
    I move forward aimlessly.

~~~~~~~~~~~~~~~~~~~~~~~~

She disguises herself as love
    but love isn't jealous,
nor does it grow poisonous.

~~~~~~~~~~~~~~~~~~~~~~~~

I don't know what you want from me
   because it's clearly not my company.
Do you enjoy knowing I want you?
   The games continue...

I don't know what I want from you.
Maybe it's just your body,
but our words are past due.
I enjoy thinking of you thinking of me,
   but, I'd rather us be touching.

We say we'll just be friends
   but the tension is tense.
   We both know we can't resist –
I can't think of you without your lips on me.
   Trying to refrain is like trying
      not to breathe.

~~~~~~~~~~~~~~

There is something

    about you

that takes my breath away.

    Forget the heart,

    my lungs are

    ... yours.

~~~~~~~~~

Last night,

you asked me what my favorite flower was.

I told you where it grows

but I never gave its name.

I was afraid to explain.

I grew nervous of further questioning...

Would I had given myself away?

Knowing me, I'd say too much.

Given my history, you'd fall for me

in too much of a rush.

I know the pattern

so I'd rather keep hushed,

'cause once you draw too close...

you'll see the intricate, beautiful

designs engraved, so carefully,

on the fine china that I am

and, you'll realize...

I'm too fragile,

too intentional.

~~~~~~~

I can't blame the weak-minded
    sometimes; there's no defense
        to suffice the pain.
There's no compensation
    for what lies slain.

~~~~~~~~~~~

Well, I guess someone's got to hold the mountains.
Don't worry,
    we can place them on my shoulders.

~~~~~~~~~~~~~~~~~~~

If I would have known
   that the last time
      the butterflies flew ...
was the last time I'd kiss you,
I'd have removed the very ground
   from beneath my feet
      so that they never would have landed.
I'd have caught every grain of sand
   to freeze the hands of time
so that I could have felt
   your lips on mine,
      with butterflies, ever, in flight.
I was willing to fall
   willing to fight,
      just so the butterflies could fly.

But I'd rather see you rise,
   see you shine
      without me,
than give flight to those butterflies.

I hope you find your wings.
I pray you find your peace.

~~~~~~~~~~~~~~~~~~~~

If you lost your way,
check your purse
    and search your mind.
If it's not there,
check your pockets
    and search your heart.
It can't be far
You just had it this morning.
Don't worry, Love...
I believe in you.

~~~~~~~~~~~

I have no pride left in me

... when it comes to you.

I'd lay it all down

just for you to walk on,

if that meant

you'd cross safely to where you're going.

And I'd spill my heart out along with these words

just so you'd never have to question

    if someone loved you.

'Cause

my heart is your own personal songbird.

I'm caged in your grasp.

I'm far from figured out,
you're far from figured out.
We met at the wrong time.
Maybe we'll meet again.

Maybe when I've grown,
maybe when you've grown...
Maybe if we cross paths in the future
we can try again.

~~~~~~~~~~~~~~~

I often find myself
    drifting
into thought
    of where this life might
        be taking you.

~~~~~~~~~~~~~~~~~

As of now,

I don't think I'm fit for this.

I'm trying to get there.

Trust me,

I want to be that answered prayer,

but how am I supposed to sit right here

and address...

Tranquility.

I think I've known it before.

If I'm thinking of the word correctly

then what comes to my mind is peace.

And I've known peace

like England knows autumn's leaves.

Beauty...

and colors so bright that you don't think

that it's possible for them to fade.

But it comes and goes

without the discretion of me or my foes.

It's not that I welcome winter's raid,

but I've invited him

by leading my heart astray.

So once again I'll say

I'm not fit to sit here

and portray a picture
of how you're supposed to get there.

Here I go anyway,
willing to share with you
what I've learned.
Through the rise and fall,
here I am, to pour out my all-in-all,
to tell you about peace and tranquility
and hopefully I don't have it all wrong.

You see,
it doesn't come from anything I've done,
or anything I was,
or anything I will ever be.
It was always there
and it's still right here.
But I've grown calloused
and part of me just doesn't seem to care.
Another part knows that there is always hope.
and that's the part that I intend to grow,
it's just that I'm in need of Love to help me cope.
So whether you like me or not

all I ask is that you don't let
my life lessons here rot.
Don't grow so hard,
don't callous your heart
to the point that you can't acknowledge autumn's leaves,
to the point that you can't see life is good,
even if it is singing all around you.
With patience
it waits, right in front of all of our blind faces,
waiting for us to breathe ... it in.
His name, is Tranquility.

Some of you may be wondering what I could possibly
    know about callousness,
what I could possibly know about pain.
"She's naive," they say.
"She's sheltered and tame."
But let me tell you,
I am a fighter.
I've had to look my mother in her eyes
and tell her, "Mom please, don't cry. It'll be ok."
I've have had to hear her pain as she begged God,
"Please don't take my baby today!"

I've witnessed death,

but now I know, I've been blessed.

Because He has always been there,

tending to my every care.

His name, is Tranquility.

But let me remind you of the pain that really hinders, the

pain of regret,

the pain of the past that you wish you had never met.

I'm not going to sit here and tell you that I'm set.

I'm not going to pretend that I'm completely content

with where I stand.

I've made my choices,

I've listened to and obeyed temptation's voices.

I've fallen and bowed to my immoralities,

enslaved myself to my sexuality,

chained my flesh to everything earthly.

All the meanwhile,

I was thinking that I was free.

I numbed myself to the slightest breeze.

I was so far down that hole,

I never gave credit to how much my sin had control.

I numbed myself to the good,

couldn't feel the Love where I stood.

But now I'm trying to get right with my soul.

I don't want to be calloused anymore.

I want to feel whole and the areas where I bleed,

appreciate the peace and recognize the areas I need to
weed.

What a gift it is to see clearly.

What a gift it is...

His name, is Tranquility.

No one ever told me

that once the apple fell from the tree,

it can roll away.

And like I've said,

I've led my heart astray.

I cut my stem

and I fell,

then still I acted on my own self-will.

And let me say,

I rolled far down that hill.

But let me tell you what I see −

I see that Tree, uprooting itself,

willing to die to come down and save me.

He says, "Let me protect you.
Just take shelter under my leaves,
autumn is almost here."
His name, is Tranquility.

~~~~~~~~~~~~~~~~~~~~

Christians,

I see many good intentions when I am approached by you and told
the good news and what I can trust in. But when you come to me
and other LGBT+ people, just to remind us that we are going to hell
if we can't change ourselves, it is very hard to find the good news in
that. It's discouraging and heartbreaking. Some of you have told me
that it is important for you to show love in the way that you know.
You say it's bold and honest, and I agree with that. But try not to
be so hateful in the way that you love. Tell us of the way that Jesus
Loves us, and how he died for us. Say prayers of thanks for our lives
instead of prayers that make us doubt that He Loves us. Welcome
us the way that Jesus would. He doesn't welcome us to tell us how
messed up we are, He calls us forth to tell us that we're forgiven. Are
we to focus on ourselves, or on God? If you agree that our focus
should be upon Him who saves, then stop directing us to see the
things that you think are ugly.

They tell me,

"God doesn't hate you,

   He hates your sin."

And now I feel the need

   to cover up my skin,

because He must hate

   the dimples in my cheeks

      that form when I smile.

He must hate the brown in my eyes

   and my five-foot-three height.

How could He Love me

   if I am sin?

~~~~~~~~~~

I wonder what I'm missing,
   wonder what I'd see,
      if I'd never seen Him.

If He hears me
I'll never know,
   but I'm scared
of being alone.

God,
why do you leave me in this fear?
I was made to die, right?
Was it written for me to perish amongst the wicked?
Why am I scared of this ride,
... of speaking the Truth?

~~~~~~~~~~~~~~~~

If I'm going to feel lonely,
   then I'd rather be alone.
To be around so many people,
   but still left to feel like the only one in the world,
   makes me feel incapable of being whole.

~~~~~~~~~~~~~~~~

It gets to a point
    where loneliness becomes a presence of its own.
It becomes the only, tangible,
    real thing to feel
        to comprehend.
It gets to a point
    that I miss it when it's gone.
Social interactions grow awkward –
    they become heavier
        than the burden
    of isolation.
I grow more and more afraid
    every day,
of how much more real
    it will become.

~~~~~~~~~~~~~~~

I am the Pacific
off the cliffside of the Oregon coast.
I throw passion
like I throw waves of excitement,
honest and wild.
I've remained untouched

... unexplored,

craving for someone to jump,

yearning for someone to know me.

Many come to see –

  I observe them

  observing me,

    clothed in their curiosity,

    from the edge of the cliffside,

careful not to trip,

careful not to slip

into my rubicon waters.

Oh,

I don't think they know.

How could they

... when they stay in the shallows?

Oh,

I don't think they know.

  I'm left alone;

  they leave me lonely.

~~~~~~~~~~~~~~~~~~~

I see the sky is clear,
　　the air is still;
not even the wind blows here
People don't believe anything can grow
　　on this desolate land.
The coldness has numbed the soil.
I watch the land grow in bitterness as it toils...
Even the evergreen, everwhite.
The land claims but never gives...
　The surface expands
　　and the lies live.
But I,
　　alone in the presence of great emptiness,
　　trek next to the beautiful, forgotten
　　everwhites.
How I long to see them uncalloused
　　and evergreen again.
I wonder what they were like;
I wonder when the cold set in.
　But I can still see the beauty,
　and even more so,
　　I can feel it.
I know there's a depth beneath the surface.

There's been no movement in this air.
Nothing moves from here.

I know why the ocean throws tsunamis
and why the forests crave fires.
I'm waiting for a storm,
waiting to see what conspires.

Is it too late to erase
... everything I never was?
Too late to take back all the mistakes
that should have never been made?
Nothing ever remains ...
new.
Imprints are made...
They're left to feel but never see.

There's been no movement within;
there's no wind to stir up this dust
and carry it away.

I'll welcome the rain.

~~~~~~~~~~~~~~~

I never did like the way that my left eye squints when I
smile;

   Or the way that my eyebrows arch when I laugh.

But there is something so beautiful in the way I cry

... the way I bite my bottom lip when I swallow my sorrows;

Or the definition in my jaw when I clench my teeth
together.

I'm prettier when I'm low;

I look stronger in my sorrows.

It's kind of peculiar the way the world trains you to see
    what it sees.

Nobody likes ugly.

Maybe that's why everything likes to tear me down.

I wasn't trained to be happy.

I was engineered to be strong.

~~~~~~~~~~~~~~~~~

This feeling is all too familiar
    like my home catching on fire
    ... and I can't save anything
    but myself.
Instead,
    I get to watch it all burn
    with everything precious to me
    becoming feathers of ashes.
Never!
    will I let myself
    feel this way again.
Nothing!
    will be precious to me
    because I'm stuck in a sprint
        running into my eternity.
God allowed this,
    but it is His calling for me,
So,
    I obey.

~~~~~~~

We can't make them understand
and I wouldn't want them to,
'cause then it'd be too late.
　Keep them away
　　from the frame
　　　before they know.
Oh, before they know the pain.

There's an equal low to the heights
　　of things,
and oh, we know,
how we know the lonely.

The only difference being
　　I've sailed the seas
　　　and you've sailed the stars
and you know better than I
that the stars need the night
　　to be seen shining.
And although the night surrounds us both,

I can see the light you wear

  and I find myself wondering

... if only I was meant to be

   amongst the stars

    instead of the sea.

Would the night be worth embracing?

～～～～～～～～～～～

In this world,

    faith is a burden,

        where hope rests.

~~~~~~~~~~~~~~~~~~~~~~~~~~~~~~

Pain is the architect

    and I am the builder

Bruised and beaten,

    while he whips me into shape

One of the greatest teachers is Pain.

~~~~~~~~~~~~~~~~~~~~~~~~~~~~~~

If I were to walk away

then I know I'd face this with pills.

Drugged into society.

Would that give me sanity?

I'm 1,000 leagues-deep into my rationality.

I can't reach.

The air at the surface teases me,

but who's drowning, is it me?

~~~~~~~~~~~~~~~~~~~~~~~~

Endless is life itself,

    from my realm

    and to the rest of the world.

It is infinite;

a size so vast

to journ it alone, is timeless.

This lives to be a definite nirvana of mine

so please don't "tame" my eyes

    for they perceive the endless

        and the sacred.

My mind is not where my logic resides;

    in fact, it defies my sense of Truth.

But something deeper is a part of me,

or ...

    me, a part of it.

I only know it exists!

... I can only feel its presence.

~~~~~~~~~~~~~~~~~~~~~~~~

Am I nothing more than the reflection
of the perceptions
projected onto me?
I'm often lost in thought,
submerged in questions, unanswered,
wondering if sight or eyes
were irrelevant...
Would you still think I'm beautiful?

~~~~~~~~~~~~~~~

I was on fire for You! And already I feel myself draining. I
don't want this. Please, Father ... don't let me let You go. I
know I've been growing distant – I can feel it. I can easily
say that it's me being on the ship that makes me sin. But
I'm learning that it is simply just me. Speak to me, God,
and help me to listen.

~~~~~~~~~~~~~~~

I feel that a vast majority of you misrepresent God and His great Love for all of His children. And yet, you wonder why the majority of gay people leave the church... It baffles me.

I do not blame other gays for leaving the church. There is so much pain associated with the thought of God when you are made to believe that He doesn't Love you. I thought that the only way for me to move on was to either die or convince myself that God wasn't real. So I began to read books and watch apologetics favoring the atheist beliefs. Maybe if God weren't real, life wouldn't be so difficult. I wanted to leave that chapter of pain and self-hate behind me. I felt that you all made it very clear that I didn't really belong there. And I'm pretty sure that other people that have walked my path resonate with my feelings.

Vultures don't hide,
   they're waiting.
As I wrestle the demons inside,
   they're anticipating my fall.
I pray...
I pray that they can't hear my heart fading.
Keep a smile on my lips
   because my eyes can't lie.

This desert is too hot,
this mountain is too steep,
this valley is flooding,
this ocean is too deep.

Oh, I hear them whispering.
Oh, they're waiting,
   I know they're waiting.

~~~~~~~~~~~~~~~~

Father,

It seems I can count the stars
    while I wait upon your return;
like a touch
    they make themselves known.
So where are you amongst the lights?
    And
where is my faith in you?
Like gold on my string of hope,
    you exist.
Just pull me on home.

~~~~~~~~~~~~~~

Lord,

I am emptied of myself
I am waiting for You now.
There is nothing for me here;
    everything that I desire is not of here.
When can I go home to You?
You have called me, but for what reason now?
How can I be of Your service in this condition?
    This pain is becoming too much;
this loneliness, how is it a blessing?
    ...Where are you?

This morning,

I woke up from somewhere deep inside of me;

a dream saturated with both

my deepest desires ... and fears.

I almost felt too deep to resurface.

Drowning in a silver sea

that I've conjured up from my dreams

is not the way I've thought of dying,

but it only pulls me deeper as the nights progress.

Before I sleep,

I breathe deep

and anticipate having to hold my breath.

~~~~~~~~~~~~~~~~~~~~~~~~~~~~~~~~~~~~

I do not wish You to see the things that I do.

I just wish You knew

    of all of the realms

        that You exclude.

I do not know why I have entered these worlds

    for it is not something I choose.

But the Truth

    I crave,

so like waves,

        they consume me.

Reasons, I could only contemplate.

    I assume nothing.

~~~~~~~~~~~~~~~~~

Was I ever even balanced?

    It seems to me

        that my dreams ...

 outgrew

... the person I am.

Tell me,

    what's the purpose of

having dreams,

    when you can't handle them?

All I can say is,

"Be with me!"

"Be with me!"

repeatedly.

    I plead.

Heavy are my thoughts,

    paralyzed is my tongue.

All I can do

    is just be.

So just please,

    let me rest.

In Your presence,

    just let me cry.

Please don't leave me,

    not even as I sleep.

All I can say is,

"Take the reins,

    take my will and make me Yours."

repeatedly.

    My heart pours.

Because I don't know what to do anymore

    but to be still in search of Your embrace.

Please, God!

Don't test my patience a moment longer.

The pain only grows stronger.

I'm waiting to feel all You are,

    to overwhelmingly cry with relief.

Because I don't know how to not feel lonely anymore.

All I can say is,

"Jesus, Jesus, oh my Jesus!"

repeatedly,

with hands raised high,

    awaiting Your touch.

Won't you come and just breathe over me?

    Won't you absolve me?

        Forgive me?

I can't stress;

I can barely whisper,

"Lord, I yearn for peace..."

    And in my thoughts

        I finish,

"Lord, I yearn for rest,"

as I await for Your caress.

I'm no lamb in the field

    but there are wolves here.

Where is my shepherd?

    ...Death awaits.

~~~~~~~~~~~

This is a battle, but what should I truly be at war with?

Is it ok for me to accept myself?

You tell us to deny ourselves and follow you

    ... I tried.

~~~~~~~~~~~

You were my first heartbreak.

The memory of our past scars me.

Was I not dedicated?

Did I not pray fervently?

Did I not remain disciplined enough through my struggles?

Is this the part where you tell me that You never knew me?

Why do you ignore me?

Why can't You speak to me?

Is it as they say?

... that I'm not pure enough?

God,

To say You broke my heart would be too little.

You broke my hands and feet.

You penetrated the ribs that protect the sacred parts of me.

The words You never said

... were crippling.

You broke every bone.

 I was incapable of doing anything.

~~~~~~~~~~~~~~~~~~~~~~~~~~~~~~~~~~~

I wrote this after one of my hallucinations. I had an episode of sleep paralysis, which was quite typical during those days. If you didn't know, you can't find the means to move during sleep paralysis. I was on my stomach, with my face towards the entrance to my room. I saw a winged demon walk into my room and fly above me. I could feel its wings brushing against my back as it flew. I was horrified.

Jesus!

I didn't see You;
I didn't even look for You
... yet, I called your name,
as if it were nothing but a chant to cast into the air for
protection.
I didn't even look for You
yet, You came!
And the thing flying above me, left.

I can feel this chapter of my life coming to an end. I'll pack my lessons and I'll be leaving; leaving the past where it lay.

~~~~~~~~

I'm swimming on the surface.
   What's the purpose,
      when I'm on my own?
I'm at a standstill on this highway
   but I'm told there are higher ways.
I can't turn back now
and I can't remain the same...

~~~~~~~~~~~~~~~

For those of you who don't believe in a god and are reading this, I feel that you may be thinking that this is just what religion does to a person. I can't argue with that, because I was deeply affected. However, the word "religion" has such a negative connotation in society. I understand the harm that having and pushing the legalistic Christian ideologies onto another can have. Let me assure you though, my experience with God's Love has very little to do with "religion". Yes, I classify myself as a Christian, but His Love speaks so much louder to me without the interference and interpretations of the many different versions of Christianity being pushed and used to judge me. It's so easy to get caught up in questioning if you're good enough or being obedient enough. But once you stop concentrating on yourself or the people and just see God, you start to realize that it was never about you. Many people, theists and atheists, forget that religion isn't legalistic in its entirety. They forget about relationship. They forget about Love. They forget about mercy and grace. But Christianity should be, first and foremost, Love.

I had to deal with many pains and questions due to me believing that I had to be a certain way. That's not Christianity. You may come across Christians who will belittle you and make you feel unwelcome and judged. But that just means that they are lost in their own way, as we all are. They are just struggling in a different light. It took me leaving the church and distancing myself from people in general, to find that God Loves me and wants to commune with me. How ironic! I felt the need to leave the church to find God. And now, I feel completely confident and armed by His Love for me. I return with a greater understanding and no fear of what others say of me.

TRUTH

SET

FREE

DEPLOYMENT 2019

I decided to go on this walk tonight because I've been feeling anxious about finally talking to Mom. I've been trying to figure out what is best for myself, I'm sick of hating every mirror and every compliment given to me. This base looks like the outward appearance of what I've been feeling lately. So sick of seeing nothing other than CONEX boxes, I figured I would walk along the fence line so I could observe the African terrain. I've been staring at this fence, instead of what lies beyond it, for quite some time now.

I know that the border that encompasses me is meant to protect us. Yet, I feel like a prisoner. This thought seems so familiar! This feeling is nothing new to me. I guess I just never thought to think of my perspectives and beliefs as something as simple as a fence.

A fence serves more than one purpose. It can serve as the perimeter of a fort, built to protect and keep the enemy from entering. It can be used as the walls that surround a prisoner, meant to endure a sentence. But no matter what, a fence is simply a fence. It's a matter of perspective. Just like a cup can be half-full or-half empty, the substance within is marked at the same place regardless of what you see.

I saw my faith as an anchor weighing me down to the bottom of the ocean instead of something holding me steady. It condemned me. No matter how much I tried to disbelieve, He wouldn't let me go. So I was stuck with believing He was real and was ok with letting me suffer the way that I did. Before I left on my deployment, I had some very intense, conversational-like prayer sessions that led to more heartbreak than I ever dared to imagine.

"God, I have no liberty to disbelieve that You are alive and all around me. I feel like I'm literally suffocating in Your presence. It's so painful! If You say that we may know what is of You by the fruit of which is produced, then how am I

to believe that all of which I feel, is good? How can I believe that me begging to not live another day, is what You want? The only conclusion that I can come to, if You say that You are all Loving and good, is that I don't know You at all. Do I even know Your name? Are You a savior called Jesus? Are you three in One? If I can't shake the belief that you exist, then I will strip everything back. I will call you Truth instead of Jesus or Messiah. I will start from scratch, Truth. I know nothing. Show me what is real and what is of You. I will listen and grab hold of what it is that You show me."

To let go of the foundation that I was brought up on made everything feel shaky. It's a terrifying thing to step out and try to see a different way. But, I was fighting for my life. It was like accepting that my whole life was a lie and all that I ever did was a waste of time. But here I was on my new chapter, seeking Truth. It wasn't very long 'til I saw Christianity in a new light. It was never God projecting hate and telling me that I was in the wrong, that He couldn't Love me: it was the people and myself. I let that sink in so deep that I couldn't see another way.

I now choose to see His Love as protection, not imprisonment! His Love is freeing, wild, and without definition. He speaks through the most unlikely of people. He is within me and every person. Every good is of Him! Christians, you are not the only ones whom He uses; He truly is everywhere. He is not a fence that imprisons, only the beliefs that you limit Him to. So don't let your beliefs prevent you from seeing and loving all of humanity and the world. Not all atheists, homosexuals and people of other faiths are evil.

As for those who don't believe in God, don't let your beliefs prevent you from seeing that Christians aren't all ridiculously, judgmental and unaccepting. Don't let your beliefs keep you from thinking that you can't have a relationship with Him.

After all, people are, simply, people.

The days blur together on deployment. After the first month or so, you start to lose track of the days as you lose a grasp on what's real, on what's waiting for you back home. During my first two deployments, I was nineteen and twenty-two. So young and so much to learn, I grew more and more unsure of myself. As I sailed the seas, on what felt like a floating prison at times, over to Europe and the Middle East, I never knew how to stop and see myself the way that I wanted others to. However, my last deployment in Africa, boots on ground, was so different. I was twenty-five: I grew to know myself; I grew to love myself.

After I decided that I couldn't go another day living this life of mine without talking to my mom, I planned to call her and finally get it off of my chest. All that was in question was what I would say to her. And of course, there was what could be said or felt on her side. I was so scared to tell her when I was younger, but at this point in my life ... that just wasn't the case. I knew that nothing could stop her loving me. I was scared of her hurting for me; of her feeling guilty that I never came to her sooner. I didn't want for her to feel like I ever questioned her love for me. After all, I also had a little brother who came out about two years before I did.

It was just like any other deployment night after my shift, but I was shaking as I went to call her. Part of me was hoping that she wouldn't answer, but she did. I could tell that she was in the car.

"Hey babe! What ya doin', booga?" her cheerful voice said.

"Just getting off of work; thought I'd call. But Mom, I need to ask you something..." I said, as I began to confront one of my biggest fears.

"Okay, mija ... what is it?"

"How long have you known about me?"

She paused for a good five seconds. "What do you mean?"

Praying that she would know what I was trying to say if I

repeated myself, I asked again, "Like, how long have you known ... *about me?*"

"Oh, we're doing this now?"

"I really need to do this now."

To my relief, she answered my question: "Probably about five years now."

"Why didn't you ever say anything or ask me?"

Quite puzzled, she told me: "Mija, I didn't think I was supposed to."

There was a silence in the air that allowed me to contemplate the fact that she hadn't hung up the phone or broken my heart somehow. I mean, I never expected her to disown me or anything, but the fact that she was still there ... wanting to hold me through the phone, assured me that everything was going to be ok.

"Cerena, I will always love you." Mom started to sniffle and then continued: "Why didn't you tell me sooner?"

"Mom, it wasn't that I was scared of telling you because of you. I have always been afraid of it all being true. And I knew that if I told you, it was because it is. I'm gay. I never thought I'd have to admit to it."

"Well Mija, as you hang up the phone right now, I want you to take a deep breath and smile. Just smile. I want you to take in, feel, and enjoy the relief of finally telling me. I love you so much!"

I was so choked up. I felt like chains that had bound me down for years in the dark, had fallen; I was able to breathe for the first time, as me. After I hung up the phone, I immediately started talking to God and commenting on the fact that my mom must have been planning and practising that response for years. Because, goodness! I couldn't have asked for it to go any better than the way that it did.

I found a glimpse of myself
in the night,
just me and the sky,
   only the moon and the stars,
     no artificial light.

~~~~~~~~~~~~~~~~~~

I will not let their perspectives of me become my reality.
I am proud of the person that I've grown into.
I believe that God has shaped me into all that I am today.
Their opinions have no value any longer!
But I am grateful for all of the heartaches,
    for all of my pain from the past,
because without all of it
the person I am wouldn't exist.

~~~~~~~~~~~~~~~~~~

Ignorance and conceit open the doors of our struggles.

And by some miracle,

   out walk faith and humility.

Books and stories may offer us knowledge

but it seems to be only by walking with fear, pain, and

suffering

...will we ever get a taste of Wisdom.

~~~~~~~~~~~~~~~~~~~~~~~~~

Wisdom,

You were more like the color of my eyes,
like the texture of my hair.
I never knew you as I knew the wind,
    or as I knew a friend,
but when you fled ...
    it felt as though
I had lost my ears
    or my mind.
Then I thought that maybe
    I had taken my ability
        to comprehend
        for granted.
But in fact,
    you have never been anything
        for anyone to claim.
Rather, by Grace, you'd visit me,
and you'd unlock doors to every circumstance that I would
    had never seen without you.
And you'd whisper things of Truth to me,
    things that I am incapable of thinking
        without you.

~~~~~~~~~~~~~~~~

My sin was fear...

    Fear,

the real obstacle that I faced.

Like a Trojan horse,

    it crept into my life

    in the shape of my sexuality,

and I let it get in the way of me

       ... and God.

It covered me, like scales,

and calloused me to His word.

~~~~~~~~~~~~~~~~~

Your words fall on me
    gracefully,
like snow,
like they don't abide by the laws of gravity;
because they don't apply to this world.
They lift me!
    And here I go again
        flying on the wings of Your promises.

~~~~~~~~~~~~~~~~~~~~~~~~~~~

Only in humility is there victory.
Only in wisdom is there humility.
And only in knowledge is there wisdom.

But where does the desire to learn and grow begin?
Through pain, sorrow, isolation.
Through strife, it seems ...
is the only way to victory in life.

You can toil through life without strife,
but only a fool's profit would be gained.
Though a blessing it is, to be without trouble.
Do not remain in oblivion.
And though a blessing, it is, to have troubles
... only through prevailing will a blessing
such as this
be complete.

So, better it is to persevere through strife and attain
victory,
than it is to work without struggle
and become a wealthy fool.

Have you ever felt like you were living in a dream;

like you believed in something that swept you away?

Have you ever given up the right to have control

  to see where the current takes you?

It's a zero-gravity kind of feeling

... in a wonderful, colorful storm,

in a "paradigm shift" reality.

It's a "how did I live without this?" kind of belief.

An "I can really just be?" kind of relief.

~~~~~~~~~~~~~~~~~~~~~~~~~~~~~~

I am every word I've spoken;
   a piece of every person
   I've ever loved;
flawed and broken,
   and then buffed.
I am an extension
   of the land I've walked,
smooth and steep.
I am enough,
   not everything,
but,
   born and killed,
and born again,
by what I experience.
I am made new
   by everything
placed under the sun,
under the moon.

~~~~~~~~~~~~~

It's not about me or you.

It's about God!

And some may say that it is about us

    as one,

        unified!

But ...

    it has to be bigger,

there just has to be more.

I refuse to believe that it's all only as great

    as I can comprehend or perceive.

I have been given Grace through humility

    and have realized,

        that I am merely a piece;

a piece of all of us,

    of our story,

        and our story,

    a piece of His story.

And if this is all True

    as I presume,

then we all must share One Truth

    because we are not divided!

Why can't you see

    there is no "my Truth"

or "your Truth"?
There is only Truth... One!
Although unknown is the whole story,
I know that it can only be Great.
Oh,
    what Glory!

All of our lives feed into One,
like springs feed the rivers,
    and rivers the lakes, and
        submerge into the sea.
All of our lives feed into One,
    and if they haven't
        have they even begun?

We are meant to intertwine;
    our lives are for each other.
So feed into mine
    as I tangle into yours.

Even if you were only a chapter of my story,
    or even just a page,
        or as simple as a word,

You are forever a part of my life story
    and no one can change that.
As it was in the beginning and is now
    and ever shall be already written.
You see, we are already a part of Him,
    and He, a part of us.
We were already chosen by Him,
    and for Him!
We are history, we are His story!

It's not about me or you,
    it's about God!

~~~~~~~~~~~~~~~~~~

Your life is a gift to mine,
    a promise and hope for relation.
Forever to be ...
    a vocation for Truth!

~~~~~~~~~~~~~~~~~~

Our veins are rivers
running for a purpose,
    flowing for a cause.
Our current remains
    but we are in constant change,
destined to never be the same.
Every second
    we are a new creation
... growing,
flowing,
towards the ocean we are destined for.

We were made to test our limits,
    coals destined to be diamonds.
Welcome the pressure,
accept the pain!
Kerosene flows through our veins
    and when passion sparks inside of us,
it sets us to flame.
Like a fire, we'll burn,
    my friend.
    Pressure breaks chains.

~~~~~~~~~~~~~~~~

After a year and some time overseas on deployment, I finally saw my parents. I'm not going to lie, I was a bit nervous. I came back from deployment a new woman in many ways: I came back feeling confident, like a lioness that didn't take bullshit from anyone. I didn't expect as much change to bloom within myself after coming out to them.

So many thoughts and self-realizations became more and more evident, like how I felt about God and His Love for me. I didn't realize how much that mentality affected the way I viewed the love of my parents. I could never fully accept their love because I felt that they didn't, fully, know me. Through no fault of their own, there was just so much that I kept hidden. This was the way that I felt about everyone who didn't know that I was gay. And I believe this speaks volumes as to why I could never accept myself. It speaks as to why I yearned for Lyla's love and threw myself into endless work to earn it, even though I was never seen by her. There were many other short-lived attempts to find love in search of approval. I was looking for someone else to love me before I ever thought to love myself.

The day after my parents arrived in Virginia was the day we finally had to chance to really talk. We drove out to Virginia Beach that afternoon. There was a Mexican restaurant close to the beach and we sat outside facing the ocean. Of course, my parents expressed their love and pride for me, but they were also honest about not fully understanding my brother and I being gay. They approached their lack of understanding with questions about my feelings and experiences. I could feel that they just wanted for me to be happy – I am so lucky to have the support that I have in them. We talked a lot and love radiated through our conversation. But my dad asked a question that really stuck with me and made me hurt for so many people that aren't lucky enough to feel loved by the those that should love them, unconditionally.

He made a comment about how he didn't think many same-sex relationships were very healthy and wondered how I saw them. He asked me if I believed myself to be different from that. I thought about it for a moment and an answer that I didn't know that I had, rolled off of my tongue: "I agree, I think that there are so many unhealthy relationships within the gay community, but when you are brought up to believe that you're disgusting, less of a human, or a disappointment, you don't typically tend to have to best perception of yourself. And then when you find people whom you think understand you, you fall into a culture that fosters a lifestyle of chaos. I see so many gays more concentrated on sex than relationships and connection. So many end up cheating or lying. They fall into despair while they chase those who reject them, just like they chase approval from family or society. Maybe if everyone was taught to respect and love themselves just as they are, they would be more mentally stable. It's just like any other straight relationship. If someone is mentally unhealthy, it's typically difficult to produce a healthy relationship. It's just how people are. It's just people."

My response even made me think.

My parents never talked about sexuality as I was growing up; I always heard everything about it at school or church. I realized that my parents never made me feel like they wouldn't love me. To be honest, I don't think my dad really cared if I were straight or gay, he just didn't understand because he couldn't relate. My mom, being Christian as well, only ever gave love and acceptance to everyone. I knew they would love me. It was always me that couldn't accept myself for being gay. I wanted to be a model Christian but I was so mentally messed up. I had no self-respect and was incapable of being in a healthy relationship. I don't think I really started to change until I just owned who I was and told my parents.

I am so thankful for them just loving me for no other reason than because they just do. I am no special case in their eyes; I'm not a disappointment or an embarrassment to them. Their love requires no explanation. I am still in so much awe of the change in myself from the time that I realized all of this, to now. And I thank God that He Loves me the same.

Shields up, forts down,
  hiding from war
  doesn't aid the crown.

Oh, because the cost of a lie is the Truth,
  and the price you'll pay for ignorance
  will be the best of you.
Trust me, friend ...
  the happiness within the wall is just fear in disguise,
fear of the outside.

What's a sword if not used, but a weight,
weight of fear?
Oh Dear, forfeit the barricades.

Shields up, forts down,
   hiding from war
  doesn't aid the crown.

Oh, the pain is real with plenty to endure.
Deceit lures like sirens of the sea
   and hate grows because grass attracts weeds.
Just let it be, oh let it be,
   for the harvest will set you free.

Hate is love, spoiled,
   and love is the light.
Omitted, what is light but barren?
It should be atop the mountains
   for all the world to see.
Yet, we bury them beneath their shadows
   where the flame cannot breathe.

Shields up, forts down,
hiding from war
doesn't aid the crown.

Aimlessly, I roam

  leaving pieces of my heart

  amongst the ones with whom I've grown.

But endless is my supply,

  so it seems,

though goodbye's sting never will cease

  and new beginnings always start bitter

  before they get sweet.

The memories flicker

  as the days wither,

  as if the presence lives amongst the pictures.

I'm learning to see there is ignorance in the act

  of walking into the future, consumed by the past.

  but I'm learning fast

that I can't move forward,

looking back.

~~~~~~~~~~

Living lies that fly past a torn sky of betrayal and deceit
to the defamation of all Truth that cracks the slandered
    earth at your feet.
Is it not the breath of man that contaminates the air
    in between,
or is it as though the poisoned air is what we breathe?
In either case, I see the self-righteous to be infected
and the humble ones, sheltered or somehow fortified,
but nonetheless protected.
Because not from their eyes do they see themselves,
but something bigger they let evaluate.
This action cleanses the conscience and the fragile mind.
Though it may not heal the earth or piece back the sky,
against either cause it will retaliate.
So for the means of this war,
meditate.
Don't just self-evaluate.

People think the blind are those who can't see beauty, but it is really those who cannot feel its presence.

~~~~~~~~~~~~~~~~~~~~~~~~~~~~~~~~

The only things worth living for in this life are down paths that we fear. Not to give into fear, but to conquer it. These paths stem from a perspective of faith. There is no adventure in trusting in what is seen.

Only in what is uncertain can you be certain in your faith, and in yourself. No other thing can make your heart beat like that. Nothing else can make every sense that you have, more keen than the moment before.

Love is passion.
But friend, passion is far from Love.

~~~~~~~~~~~~~~~~~~~~~~~

In our richest forms
  we are passionate beings.
All that is,
  all that exists
... they all hold seasoned beauty.
But they see us
  and they know,
they know
who we are.

We are beyond the physicalities...
  There is something within us
    that surpasses our mentalities.

~~~~~~~~~~~~~~~~~~~~~~~

The strongest people are the ones who know their
   own weaknesses,
while the weakest people are those who are consumed
   by their own strengths!

~~~~~~~~~~~~~~~~~~

The breaths I take following these words are not owed to me... They are not something that I will earn or be rewarded. Rather, they are a million gifts taken for granted.

And you are guilty, as well as I, of dismaying this purpose; of ignoring the meaning for which you and I breathe, move, touch ... the depths of the very definitions of our lives. A million second chances are thrust upon the core of our existence, like a new page. In this new breath, we are cleansed, absolved. This profound genesis presents itself in every breath. In every breath! So stop and breathe, and start again. What does it mean to you ... to breathe? What is a breath?

~~~~~~~~~~~~~~~

Give me the oblivion of a breath,
and maybe then ... I'll fear death.

~~~~~~~~~~~~~~~

Tell me my limits,
But to say that I'd obey them
I can't promise that.

~~~~~~~~~~~~~~~

Maybe if I stayed,

I never would have lost myself...

Or maybe I never would have had the opportunity to
find me.

~~~~~~

Lies are the foundation of all that enslaves us.

Freedom is only found in the Truth!

~~~~~~~~~~~~~~~~~~

I didn't know who I was

... 'til I was left alone.

I didn't know what I was

… 'til I was all I had.

~~~~~~~~~

I thought I had to leave
    to find me,
as if I weren't right where I was.

~~~~~~~~~~~~~~~~~~~~~~~~~~~~~~~~~~

Is it not the obligation
  of every living thing
to be the best version of itself?
If even the flowers know to bloom,
   why do we refuse?

~~~~~~~~~~~~~~~~~~~~~~~~~~~~~~~~~~

Waking up every day to a new me, a new freedom that I could embrace shamelessly felt too good to be real. I felt like I was a little girl again. I was able to go back inside of myself and greet the "real me" that I had lost so long ago. I was excited to explore and to love whomever I wanted to. I became fearless and bold. I became the person that I always knew I was somehow.

The little girl inside of me is still growing and exploring. I've tried dating women openly and now feel free to talk to my mom about it and get her advice. I love being able to include her in who I am and what is going on with me. However, it turns out that I have some insecurities that I am still learning to address. I do not fear them though; I feel strong enough to confront them and examine their origins. The girls that I have tried dating have brought out some good and bad qualities that I was unaware that I had. I haven't had anything too serious in terms of a romantic relationship. My flings are typically short-lived. But I've learned something about myself with the two girls that I have dated. I've learned that I am patient and have a lot of perseverance. I've learned that I am quite emotionally intelligent and empathetic. I am also too sensitive and too dorky to be that sensitive. At times, I'm presented with situations that I am slow to understand and can be a bit judgmental. But, I'm loving this journey of being myself and watering the little girl that I had neglected for so long. I've forgiven myself for not knowing better, I've forgiven the Christians who made me doubt God's Love.

I know that as the days go on, I will be getting to know the world as well as myself through my true lenses. Not the lenses that a society or a culture tell me that I need to wear. I am free to love and to accept love! Thank God.

TO
CONCLUDE

The last thing I ever imagined, even a year ago.... Was to find peace with God and accept His love by learning to accept and Love myself. Yes! My gay, little self.

It was always
    through the ironics
        in my life ...
where I saw progress,
breakthroughs.
That's where I see
He works.
It's like checks and balances;
    all ways must be humble
        or be humbled.

~~~~~~

Thank you for reading a little bit about me.

I'll leave you with this...

TRUST GOD'S PLAN.

Thinking back on my life, I see that I was always striving to perfect myself, as if it were possible. I could never just trust God: I lived in fear of Him and tried to take matters into my own hands to, maybe, earn His Love. I was always hearing about how His Love is given graciously because no one can earn it. But, I don't think that I ever really did believe that – I knew it, but I never allowed myself to feel it. So there I went, trying to win Him over.

But what I've grown to understand is that rejecting who you are isn't necessarily denying yourself, at least in the way the Bible might mean it. I may be wrong – I am no theologian – but, in my case, I feel that God needed me to learn something. I needed to deny my own works, deny my capability of earning His Love, deny myself the power to save my own life. It was never a burden that was meant for me to carry.

I can already hear my fellow Christians agreeing and then following up with the argument that none of this means that I have to be gay. And to those of you might be saying that, I will say this: I've never wanted to be gay. In fact, I wish I weren't. It's made my life so difficult. As my brother and I would say, if there were a magic pill that could make me straight, I'd be taking it. Being gay isn't a choice, trust me. I know many of you disagree but think about it.

Say there was man, and someone told him that to not be attracted to the woman that he was attracted to. How do you suppose that he were to go about that? You can't change how you feel. I've tried dating men; I've tried praying my "gayness" away and I've hated myself. That was the most prominent thing that grew from me trying to be straight.

I will agree to the accusation of me being sexually immoral. Whether that has to do with me being gay or not, I am no more or less sexually immoral than the next person. People tell me that my battle, or thorn in my flesh if you will, is the fact that I will have to remain single for the rest of my life. For those of you that push that ideology onto people like myself, I feel that it is more than unfair. I know that being single is something that is celebrated. According to Paul the prophet, it is better, even. And at the moment, I embrace being single. But it should be a choice – that's the beauty of it. For you to say that I'm the exception and that those are the cards I was dealt, is ignorant in my opinion. Truly, I mean no offense.

As much as I wish that I weren't gay, I am thankful for the life lessons and answers that it threw me in search of. Without this journey, I don't think that I would have ever grown to see what I do now. I can rest in the Love that God has for me. I can trust that He has a plan.

I've always been divided into many, very different, pieces. Some parts of me I find in solitude, and other parts I find within all of the people that have walked the halls of my life. And I'm grateful for every lonely moment, every friend or stranger, and every obstacle that brought about all of the pain I've endured. For many years, I've lived in fear that comes along with the territory of being gay and loving God. For those who still don't know, this battle feels like a matter of life and death when you're going through it. Learning to love myself and accepting the Love that God has for me was the way for me to choose life. So here I stand today

... THAT GAY CHRISTIAN GIRL.

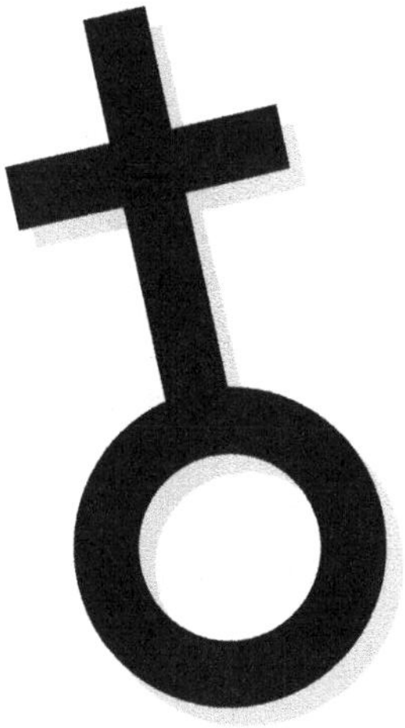

ACKNOWLEDGEMENTS

I'd like to thank;

My siblings Cassie, Jackie and Steven and my cousin Sonya for their amazing and unconditional support.

My parents for loving me and cherishing who I am. I've grown to realize just how lucky I am to have the parents that I do. Their love helped me to love myself.

God, for never letting me go. For being my anchor in the storm.

Made in United States
North Haven, CT
19 January 2023

31295753R00095